I0470976

Business Leadership Lessons from Paul the Apostle:

Tips for Organizational Success from One of History's Greatest Leaders

By Leo Wiltshire, M. A. in
Organizational Leadership

Preface by
Kathleen A. Patterson, Ph.D.

Edited by
Joy Henley, *Inkstained Editing*

Design and Layout by
Eileen DesAutels Wiltshire, M. Ed.

ISBN-10: 1492252484
ISBN-13: 978-1492252481

DEDICATION

For just about all of us, our first exposure to leadership comes from our parents. With that in mind, Eileen and I would like to dedicate this text to our parents: Leo & Katherine Wiltshire and Paul & Sue-Joan DesAutels.

TABLE OF CONTENTS

ACKNOWLEDGEMENTS

I wish to acknowledge and thank the faculty, staff, and students that I met, studied under and with, and worked with at Regent University. You all inspired me to put forth my best effort, which I hope shows in this text. I also thank my wife, Eileen, for her love and devotion. I truly thank my Lord and Savior, Jesus of Nazareth, for His generous provision.

PREFACE

When asked to write this forward, I felt honored. Not because Leo thought that I should be the one to write it, but because of the message and meaning in the manuscript.

I have had the good pleasure of watching Leo progress in his writing and scholarship, and with his love of servant leadership and the Apostle Paul. And then to see him write this manuscript on the topics that have become so dear to him.

Paul's leadership has been the topic of a tremendous amount of discussion, a topic that I am sure will never grow old, as we try to understand both leadership and Paul and take the lessons observed from scripture. What was it about Paul that made him so compelling in both Biblical days and today. Leo does a wonderful job of extrapolating the leadership lessons from Paul and discussing them in light of the modern world.

The primary components that Leo looks at with Paul are: Humility, Contentment, Compassion, Conflict, Character and Service. The value of this manuscript is not only the deeper understanding of Paul's leadership, but also the look into how these principles work in today's world.

With all the corruptions, scandals, and dramas that we see playing out in the leadership realm today, it is refreshing to look at these characteristics that are foundational to any leader desiring more from their own leadership. My prayer is that those who read this manuscript are blessed by the insights provided and find a more meaningful journey as a leader.

All the best.

— Dr. Kathleen A. Patterson

PROLOGUE

This book is intended to be an encouraging introduction to ethical and inspirational organizational leadership techniques. Too many modern-day leaders struggle to stay on a path that will properly motivate followers and set an example for other leaders to emulate. Leaders' focus on personal power and self gratification cannot be considered to be an effective way to inspire employees to put forth their best efforts to serve and develop their organizations.

Each chapter of this work will provide its information in three parts. The first part will focus on the leadership of Paul the Apostle, spotlighting either an event that occurred during his ministry or something he wrote about in his epistles. An attempt will be made to link the significance of Paul's experience or writing to modern day leadership. I have selected to focus on Paul because of the circumstances of his early life which highlight the fact that anyone has the potential to be a great leader. Paul's story has, and will continue to, withstand the test of time.

The second part of each lesson segment will focus on a leadership theory, practice, or teaching that I have learned during my experiences in graduate school. The text will focus on something I have learned that I feel has great significance for today's leaders. The purpose of this section is to call the attention of leaders to important practices that they may already be aware of, but may not be practicing effectively.

The third section will spotlight a modern-day leader whom I feel has displayed leadership qualities that Paul would approve of. Those qualities would include looking out for the well-being of others, taking responsibility for personal behavior, and displaying humility. This section is meant to signify to leaders that there are others in the modern world who are setting a positive example and that every leader could learn from, and easily follow, those examples.

I believe that this work will impact the actions of persons in leadership roles by encouraging new behaviors that will encourage other leaders to do likewise, and inspire followers and employees to work in the best interests of their organizations. Among the concepts that this work should impact are leadership development, values, and organizational performance. This book seeks to present itself as a training tool. New to this presentation of the material are thought-provoking questions for private reflection or discussion in groups.

One point I struggled with during the writing of this text was its tone. Would I be coming across as too preachy? After much internal debate, I decided to stick with the writing as my inner feelings dictated. The message contained within is of vital importance to leaders and if I got a bit emotional while delivering it, then so be it! Legacies are at stake. Leaders have to decide how they want to be remembered by others after they are gone. The point of this text is to help them make that decision.

A large part of why I desired to complete the Master of Arts in Organizational Leadership program was because I had spent a considerable amount of my previous career working for supervisors who did not utilize proper motivational techniques. I desired to learn appropriate leadership techniques in order to assist other leaders in improving their own leadership skills. I believe this text, *Business Leadership Lessons from Paul the Apostle*, will inspire organizational leaders to act as leaders, coaches, and mentors to their followers, and not merely as bosses or managers. This inspired change in the ways leaders supervise their employees should motivate those employees to perform their tasks in a manner that will increase their productivity to the organization and provide multiple benefits to their own level of personal job satisfaction.

INTRODUCTION

I present myself here before you as a man who has had to re-invent himself because my previous life was no longer working for me. I was meandering through my life pursuing my temptations and a notion of what, at the time, I believed to be a measure of success on a personal level. One of my desires was to have people look up to me, to think of me as an outstanding leader. I wanted the people I worked with to do what I told them to because I had a job title and the responsibility of running a business upon my shoulders. I wanted to be a leader! In many ways, I was a great leader and manager. But, in many ways, what I was doing on the job was not enough. I was missing a mentor to help point me in the proper direction and assist me to develop the people skills I needed to be a great leader. I have since then found that mentor. His writings mark some of the most important teachings in the best book ever written on leadership, the Holy Bible.

I suppose that some of you may be thinking; "So what does anything in the Bible have to do with organizational leadership of today? People in the Bible can't relate to anything people are doing now, can they?" It's true that Moses didn't have a laptop computer. Jesus never missed

His flight to New York. When Judas went to call the Roman guard to the Garden of Gethsemane, he didn't exclaim "There's no cellular signal in this part of Jerusalem! I'll have to deliver my information to the High Priests in person! TAXI!!!" Heck, we're now coming down to the last surviving members of a generation who had to physically stand up, walk across the room, and turn a knob in order to change the channel on their TV! How are you relating to *them*? How can anyone in the Bible relate to what we're doing now? Because in modern-day, just as in Biblical times, we all have to deal with other people. That is what this is all about. It is about dealing with people. It is about personal relationships with others. It is about setting a good example for others to follow. That is a relevant topic in any age!

Sadly, modern-day leadership is in crisis. Far too many leaders are stumbling into temptation, destroying their careers, and setting a poor example for others. Since the nature of leadership is a relationship of influence between leaders and followers, a fallen leader can cause harm not only to themselves, but also to their followers and their organizations. Dr. Richard Daft defined leadership as "an influence relationship among leaders and followers who intend real changes and outcomes that reflect their shared purposes."[i] Over the past few years, news headlines have carried multiple stories of leaders who have listed false credentials on their resumes and fathered children outside of their marriages. I consider it to be highly doubtful that any follower would consider that type of behavior to be a shared purpose.

The fact of the matter is that, whether we are leaders or followers, every one of us is human and therefore subject to falling victim to our temptations. Authors Gary McIntosh and Samuel Rima wrote, "When we refuse to process in healthy ways feelings of insecurity, unhealthy codependence issues, feelings of personal shame, deeply sublimated anger or fear, or some combination of these or other issues, they will wreak havoc in our lives and leadership and eventually endanger ourselves and others."[ii] We are seeing too many leaders being dragged down by their inability to control the most basic of human emotions and much wreckage is left behind for the world to see. When that happens, it can be a formidable task for the leader to bounce back. Fortunately, although formidable, the task is not impossible.

This teaching is meant to be a work of inspiration for leaders and followers. For leaders to draw inspiration from others who have set a good example to follow, and for followers to know that good leaders are out in the world, they just may be a little harder to find. The works and teachings of an influential leader from the past will be examined. Modern day leadership theories and teachings will be presented and discussed, along with their implications for modern-day leaders. Finally, each of the six chapters in this teaching will spotlight a modern-day leader who I feel personifies the qualities of the previously discussed past influential leader. It is my sincere hope that all readers will find the leaders profiled in these chapters to be uplifting examples of the best aspects of leadership. Great leaders can come from anywhere, and from any set of circumstances. Great leaders can even come from the path of redemption and reinvention.

This influential leader from the past was himself in need of redemption from the atrocities he was committing and was about to commit. With mentoring, he was reinvented and because of his leadership his influence reaches us in this modern-day era, almost 2,000 years after his execution. This leader is known as Paul of Tarsus, also known as Paul the Apostle, or St. Paul. Paul's story begins as one of redemption. He was originally known as Saul, a citizen of Rome and an educated Jewish Pharisee. Saul persecuted the earliest followers of Christianity. As the Book of Acts recorded, "At that time the church in Jerusalem suffered terribly. All of the Lord's followers, except the apostles, were scattered everywhere in Judea and Sumaria. Saul started making a lot of trouble for the church. He went from house to house, arresting men and women and putting them in jail" (Acts 8:1-3). So Saul was arresting people because of their religious beliefs. If he had remained on this path, we might only be remembering him today as a bigot or a common thug. However, his redemption and reinvention allowed him a chance to right his actions, and become a man who I feel is one of the greatest leaders this world has ever known.

From the story of Paul, men and women in leadership positions can find inspiration and guidance to become the best leaders for their followers that they can be. With inspiring leaders to guide them, followers can be more productive in their effort to achieve and exceed the goals of their organizations. And leaders and organizations that exceed their goals can set the example for others to follow. Ladies and gentlemen: Paul has some advice for you!

CHAPTER I: HUMILITY

The story of Paul the Apostle is one of redemption. Originally, he was known throughout his society as Saul, and Saul was in serious need of redemption. As the overly-enthusiastic Jewish Pharisee he was, Saul persecuted the followers of the then newly-established Christian movement. He had people, men and women both, thrown into prison. He gave his blessing to the stoning of Stephen. And it is possible that Saul may have arranged to have his victims flogged.[iii]

In his letters, he admits he did some bad things although he avoids specifics. In Galatians he recorded, "I was a much better Jew than anyone else my own age, and I obeyed every law that our ancestors had given us" (Gal. 1:14). And in 1 Corinthians, "I am the least important of all the apostles. In fact, I caused so much trouble for God's church that I don't even deserve to be called an apostle" (1 Cor. 15:9). In Acts, Paul spoke of his prior misdeeds and acknowledged witnesses to them, "I made trouble for everyone who followed the Lord's way, and I even had some of them killed. I had others arrested and put in jail. I didn't care if they were men or women. The high priest and all the council members can tell you that this is true" (Acts 22:4-5). Without redemption, Saul would have gone down in history as a bigot, a thug, and possibly even worse!

The book of Acts tells us Saul's redemption began when he was on his way to Damascus. He was intent on arresting any followers of the Christian movement he found there and bringing them to Jerusalem to be punished. Saul even had documents from the high priest giving him authority to take prisoner any followers of the Way who he found. So here was Saul, about to enter Damascus with all this power and authority, probably thinking he was all that, a bag of chips, and a 32-ounce soda, when all of a sudden...he gets smacked down! He was thrown from his horse, blinded by a flash of light, and told by a Higher Authority, "You work for me now, mister!" (Acts 9:1-9). And thus began Paul's journey toward becoming a true leader. He believed his own hype, and he was humbled for doing so. The word I want to discuss in this lesson is *humility*. Saul's redemption could not have happened without him having received humility and accepting it.

The word humility could easily be confused with the

word humiliation. The Oxford Dictionary defines humility with words like, "Humbleness, modesty, and meekness."[iv] However, those are words that easily could describe a servant leader. Servant-leadership was a phrase first used by scholar Robert Greenleaf in 1970. Greenleaf believed, "True leadership emerges from those whose primary motivation is a deep desire to help others."[v] In other words, servant-leaders are more focused on building up others than themselves. Leaders humble themselves and serve their organization by helping others to be successful. Servant-leaders practice what is referred to in Greek as *agapao* love. Bruce Winston wrote that *agapao* love "refers to a moral love, doing the right thing at the right time for the right reason...to love in a social or moral sense."[vi] Servant-leaders make it a point to *love thy neighbor.*

While the discussion of servant-leadership is recent, the concept of it is not. Jesus was recorded describing it in the Gospel of Matthew, where He said, "Whoever wants to become great among you must be your servant, and whoever wants to be first must be your slave—just as the Son of Man did not come to be served, but to serve, and to give his life as a ransom for many" (Matt. 20:26-28). Contrast these words of Jesus with these words taken from a Forbes article: "Compensation for the chief executives of America's biggest corporations is way up in 2011, 28 percent higher than last year on average, according to Governance Metrics International."[vii] Consider this question: What if someone is working in a position of leadership solely in order to enrich themselves monetarily? Granted, good leaders should be rewarded for their efforts, just as good followers should be. But if the people in charge claim potentially excessive rewards for themselves while followers are being laid-off, having their workloads increased, or their compensation cut, can that person be considered a good leader? Larry Spears wrote, "Servant-leadership holds that the primary purpose of a business should be to create a positive impact on its employees and community, rather than using profit as the sole motive."[viii] One needs to look no further than the examples of Jesus to understand the true definition of the servant as leader concept. From feeding 5,000 followers, to foot washing, to His death on the cross, Jesus modeled love, humility, and sacrifice and He did it all…without a paycheck!

Servant leadership was practiced in modern day by General Peter Chiarelli. General Peter Chiarelli, recently retired, was in attendance at a Washington, D. C., dinner party in early 2011. A White House consultant who was seated, and only saw General Chiarelli's striped pants, mistook him for a waiter and asked him to get her a glass of wine[ix]. The four-star General Chiarelli, who was then "the Army's second highest-ranking general,"[x] made himself a servant and retrieved a glass of wine for the consultant. After 40 years of service and having reached the highest echelon of power in the mightiest military in the world, it is doubtful anyone would have begrudged General Chiarelli if he had simply ignored the request or even berated the person who made it. He did neither. Kathleen Patterson wrote, "Servant leaders look for an attitude of humility and modesty along with selflessness and altruism, an approach which seeks what is best for others rather than for the leader personally."[xi] Rather than taking offense, General Chiarelli found humor in the moment.

After good naturedly serving the wine, General Chiarelli was quoted as saying, "It was an honest mistake that anyone could have made. She was sitting, I was standing and walking behind her, and all she saw were the two stripes on my pants, which were almost identical to the waiters' pants."[xii] So, he found humor in the unexpected situation at hand, humbled himself, and made national headlines because of his humility. It was definitely not a bad night out for General Chiarelli.

Consider this fact that, as a leader, you are doing a job. A big part of that job is to provide direction to the people who toil under your leadership. Do not be fooled into thinking that your position as leader makes you greater or more important that those you are directing. We are all just human beings walking this earth for a brief period of time. Yes, you may be thought of as a great leader and, if you are, that is truly commendable. But that greatness is to be bestowed upon you by others. To bestow greatness upon yourself is...well...let us just agree that it is not something that truly great leaders do.

Questions for Discussion or Contemplation

1. Think of an example of a leader whom you feel could do a better job of leading by demonstrating humility. What could they improve on?

2. Is there ever a time or circumstance where a leader is able to think of themselves as great?

3. Who do you see and admire for practicing servant-leadership? What do they do to set an example for other leaders?

4. What do you do to demonstrate servant-leadership to others?

CHAPTER II: CONTENTMENT

Saul, later known as Paul the Apostle, was humbled while on his way to Damascus. Instead of arresting followers of the Christian Way as he intended, he spent his time in Damascus preaching alongside them. The Book of Acts recorded, "For several days Saul stayed with the Lord's followers in Damascus. Soon he went to the Jewish meeting places and started telling people that Jesus is the Son of God" (Acts 9:19-20). Thus began Saul's new life as a leader within the very movement he previously so desperately wanted to destroy.

Shortly after joining the Apostles, Saul became known as

Paul, and he was sent out with Barnabas on missions to help spread the Word. While he was out on those missions, Paul became a victim of the same persecution he had previously inflicted on others. Paul was stoned (Acts 14:19), whipped, and imprisoned (Acts 16:22-23) for preaching the Word. But he let nothing get in the way of what he needed to do. Paul was determined to press on at his mission regardless of his personal circumstances, even if those circumstances meant that he was in prison.

Paul wrote some very important letters while he was in prison. He makes his situation obvious in his letters. In one letter he wrote, "The Roman Guards and all the others know that I am here in jail because I serve Christ" (Philippians. 1:13). In another letter he recorded, "But I would rather ask you to do it simply because of love. Yes, as someone in jail for Christ. I beg you to help Onesimus! He is like a son to me because I led him to Christ here in jail" (Philemon 1:9-10). And this passage from 2 Corinthians almost reads like a shopping list, as Paul wrote:

> I have worked harder and have been put in jail more times. I have been beaten with whips more and have been in danger of death more often. Five times the Jews gave me thirty-nine lashes with a whip. Three times the Romans beat me with a big stick, and once my enemies stoned me. I have been shipwrecked three times, and I even had to spend a night and a day in the sea (2 Cor. 11:23-25).

And you think you had a bad week at your job because a customer yelled at you?

Paul wrote something that is very significant for modern-day leaders in one of his letters. This particular passage from Philippians reads:

> I am not complaining about having too little. I have learned to be satisfied with whatever I have. I know what it is to be poor or to have plenty, and I have lived under all kinds of conditions. I know what it means to be full or to be hungry, to have too much or too little. Christ gives me the strength to face anything (Philippians 4:11-13).

Contrast Paul's words with the guy you're listening to in the next cubicle who sounds like he is ready to burst a blood vessel because the vending machine is sold out of potato chips. Paul was as focused as a laser beam in doing what he needed to get done because he learned how to be content, no matter what was happening around him, no matter what was being done to him. Can any of us say that we are so focused in completing our tasks? I know I can't. While writing these lessons, I had two cats constantly crying for my attention. Once they had succeeded in distracting me, I figured I'm already distracted...might as well check out the internet for a few minutes! I was discontent; Paul was not. He was able to keep going, to keep working toward his purpose, even if he was in prison. He found contentment in all situations and through contentment he gained focus. Can you just imagine what you could do for your organization if you were as content and focused as Paul?

Hopefully, you as a leader will never be in the positions that Paul was placed in. So, since the threat of being thrown in prison and beaten for your beliefs has been taken off the table, why not consider what could happen if everyone in your office was as content and as focused on the purpose as Paul was? The tone of the office is set by the leader. Are you providing an environment that allows your people to work at full efficiency? That cannot happen if conflicts and distractions within the organization are not addressed. Bruce Winston wrote, "To make and sustain peace is an exacting, labor-intensive process. Peace does not occur because we do nothing. Peace is not an absence of strife. Peace is something that we maintain."[xiii] The leader must work at creating, and then maintaining, a work environment that promotes peace within the organization.

How does a leader maintain peace within an organization? The most important thing for the leader to do is lead by example. If you need your people to concentrate on their task, the leader must stay on task as well. Blanchard and Hodges observed that, "Jesus stayed on point. He did not seek to take on other tasks or the agenda others hoped He would fulfill."[xiv] Many people of the day thought that Jesus would overthrow the Roman occupation of the Jewish land, but that task was not on Jesus's "to-do" list. Instead, He said, "Give the Emperor what belongs to him and give God what belongs to God" (Matthew 22:21), and He stayed on His purpose. Blanchard and Hodges reminded that, "When the going gets rough or temptations and distractions come with short-term success or setbacks, people will look to the leaders to see how they will respond."[xv] What will you, as leader, show your followers when distractions pop up within your organization?

What are those distractions? They could be in the form of ideas that do not fit with the organization's mission, a problem that was not anticipated during a project's planning stage, or an employee who is not on board with the values of the organization. In order to maintain peace, the leader must not simply ignore a problem and hope it will go away. Bruce Winston wrote, "Peace is a classic view of a system, and according to systems theory, a characteristic of a system is entropy, the slow self destruction of a system. Thus, a leader has to continually intervene to maintain peace."[xvi] For a leader, peace can be internal, like with Paul. If it is to be external, it must be maintained. Whichever the case, if you have peace, you and your organization can achieve your purpose.

Not many people may be familiar with the man who goes by the name of Tom Shadyac, but a lot of people have seen his movies. He was the director of several Jim Carrey films, such as *Ace Ventura: Pet Detective*, *Liar Liar*, and *Bruce Almighty*. He also produced of some of those films, in addition to others, including *Evan Almighty* and *I Now Pronounce You Chuck and Larry*. An article in *Christianity Today* revealed:

> Tom Shadyac, a professing Catholic who reads Augustine and Merton, was the youngest joke writer ever for Bob Hope. He graduated UCLA film school in 1989 and then worked in television for a few years before making the leap to feature films.[xvii]

Shadyac walked away from all of it: Hollywood, the money, his mansion...because it no longer suited his purpose.

His purpose was a documentary he wanted to make about why people work against each other in a system of competitiveness.[xviii] The documentary came out in 2011 and is called simply *I Am*. There are some who question such a move by Shadyac, especially since he suffered a concussion beforehand.[xix] However, Paul found his purpose in a vision while on the road to Damascus. Shadyac suffered a concussion and then Post Concussion Syndrome after a severe bicycling accident in 2007.[xx] Could his unfortunate accident be considered an enlightening experience that set him toward his purpose? Only Tom Shadyac can answer that.

Earlier in this lesson, I quoted Paul on the subject of contentment. Does Tom Shadyac understand contentment? Listen to these words from him in a 2011 interview: "The word contentment comes from the word content, which is what we hold inside—love, value, a feeling of a life that has meaning or purpose, a cause greater than yourself that you're a part of. These are the things that bring true happiness."[xxi] Mr. Shadyac's view of contentment appears to be quite sound. The film's official trailer says Mr. Shadyac set out to ask, "What's wrong with our world? What can we do about it?" At the end of the trailer, Mr. Shadyac answered, "We ended up discovering what's right with it." Did the *I Am* documentary achieve his purpose? That will be up to you to decide, should you opt to see the film. Regarding *I Am*, film critic Roger Ebert wrote:

> Like the fish, birds, animals and untouched tribes, we have evolved to cooperate and arrive at consensus. By competing to enrich ourselves, we create bad vibes. Give Shadyac credit: He sells his Pasadena mansion, starts teaching college and moves into a mobile home... Now he offers us this hopeful, if somewhat undigested, cut of his findings, in a film as watchable as a really good TV commercial, and just as deep.[xxii]

Mr. Ebert gave *I Am* two stars out of four. Of course, as

always, a film's true value is in the eye of the individual viewer.

The lesson for leaders here is that, through contentment, you and your organization can achieve your purpose and potential greatness. Contentment comes from within you. And inspiration for your purpose can come from anywhere.

Questions for Discussion or Contemplation

1. What are the things that distract you when you are attempting to focus on a task?

2. Can you name an unusual source of inspiration that provoked you or someone you know into doing a significant action?

3. What kind of emotional tone do you set for employees at your organization? How can you improve it in order to help your employees to be more productive?

4. Think of a time when circumstances in your life changed for the worse. How did you emotionally handle the situation? What, if anything, would you do to handle that situation differently now?

CHAPTER III: COMPASSION

What would you do if you were thrown into prison on charges you thought were unjust? Unfortunately, the act of imprisoning, torturing, and killing people for their beliefs is something that has been going on for thousands of years. Paul admitted to persecuting followers of the Christian movement and, as one of the movement's most vocal advocates, it was done to him. As discussed in the previous chapter, Paul found contentment within any situation he had imposed upon him. As a prisoner, he kept busy by writing letters, some of which became part of the New Testament. It was also during his time as a prisoner when

Paul got to display an example of leadership that holds a valuable lesson for modern-day leaders.

The common phrase "Let no good deed go unpunished" certainly applied to Paul and his ministry partner, Silas. For ordering a demon out of a slave girl, as recounted in chapter 16 of the Book of Acts, they were arrested, beaten, and thrown in prison. So Paul and Silas were sitting in a prison cell, their feet shackled, praying and singing to God. At about midnight, a big earthquake struck the prison. Acts recorded, "Suddenly a strong earthquake shook the jail to its foundations. The doors opened and the chains fell from all the prisoners" (Acts 16:26). What happened next is what gave Paul his chance to set an example for leaders.

Would anyone ever blame Paul for taking advantage of this opportunity to escape his dank prison cell and go back about his way? I would sure find it tempting to see how quickly I could put a few miles between myself and that prison. But Paul looked at the bigger picture. The author of Acts wrote, "When the jailer woke up and saw that the doors were open, he thought that the prisoners had escaped. He pulled out his sword and was about to kill himself" (Acts 16:27). What an opportunity Paul has here. He and Silas are imprisoned on an unjust charge and now the prison gates are open, their shackles have come undone, and the jailer is ready to kill himself. This sounds like a no-brainer to me! Run, Paul, run! Of course that did not happen. Neither Paul nor any of the other prisoners bothered to escape that night. Howard Marshall commented, "The attention shifts from the prisoners to the jailer who was roused from his sleep by the earthquake;

seeing the open doors he drew the conclusion that the prisoners had already escaped and was about to commit suicide."xxiii As a citizen of Rome, Paul most likely knew that the jailer's honor and life were at stake and he called out: "Don't harm yourself! No one has escaped" (Acts 16:28). I'm sure that the jailer could not believe his ears when he heard Paul shout out to him.

The jailer called for torches, entered the cell, and found Paul and Silas still there. Acts recorded, "After he had led them out of the jail, he asked, 'What must I do to be saved?'" (Acts 16:30). The jailer then brought Paul and Silas to his house and fed them. And Paul welcomed the jailer and his family into the faith. Paul had shown compassion for his jailer, and in return won a new convert for the Christian movement. For you, the modern-day leader, that is the equivalent of landing the new client or securing that big sale for your organization. Show compassion for others and who knows what good things can come to your reputation as a result?

Scholar Richard Daft identified four significant eras in leadership and the traits that made each of those eras unique. The first era was pre-industrial, which Daft termed "Great Person Leadership." Daft wrote, "Most organizations were small and were run by a single individual who many times hired workers because they were friends or relatives, not necessarily because of their skills or qualifications."xxiv I believe the word for this is "nepotism." The second era, "Rational Management," while environmentally stable, now requires more rules over laborers and a leader to enforce them. As Daft explained, "This era sees the rise of the 'rational manager' who directs and controls others using an impersonal approach."xxv Employees followed what this manager said, or else. Needless to say, these controlling styles of leadership are no longer suitable or effective in modern-day organizations, but that is not to imply that they are no longer in practice.

The third era identified by Daft is "Team or Lateral Leadership," and was necessitated by the evolving global business climate. Advances in communications and computing technology combined to make the world a seemingly smaller place, allowing problems and issues in one part of the world to affect another. Daft explained, "Rather than conceiving of leadership as one person being firmly 'in charge,' leadership is often shared among team leaders and members, shifting to the person with the most knowledge or expertise in the matter at hand."xxvi Rather than simply having to manage their own little portion of the world, leaders are now finding themselves having to negotiate among the chaos that abounds within the global marketplace.

Finally we come to Daft's description of this modern leadership era, "Learning Leadership." "Era 4 represents the learning leader who has made the leap to giving up control in the traditional sense. Leaders emphasize relationships and networks, and they influence others through vision and values rather than power and control."xxvii Is it not obvious to see where the model of leadership has evolved to over the past five or six generations? Organizational leaders must be able to depend upon others in order to be successful in the modern-day global marketplace. And if a leader does not show caring and compassion for others, then why should those others care about them? If people do not like the leader, they will not be receptive to that leader's vision of the future.

The leader may be able to get away with reverting back to a command-and-control model for awhile, but that will not secure the best efforts from the followers and will stifle their creativity and innovation. And then the organization will wither and die. Ken Blanchard and Phil Hodges wrote, "In an organization, if a leader does not respond to the needs and desires of his people, these folks will not take good care of their customers."xxviii As a leader, you need your people. What are you doing to make them feel valued?

Showing compassion for others is what Aaron Feuerstein did in the aftermath of a fire that devastated his family's business. Malden Mills was a textile manufacturer located in Lawrence, Massachusetts. In December 1995, fire virtually destroyed three factory buildings, threatening financial ruin to the families who depended on the business for their livelihoods. "The next day, company president Aaron Feuerstein announced that he would rebuild in Lawrence, and he promised to keep his employees on the payroll during the time it would take to reconstruct the plant."xxix Mr. Feuerstein paid his employees their salaries while the Malden Mills plant was rebuilt. That bit of generosity was not an insignificant expense. It cost him $25 million.xxx Mr. Feuerstein could have just taken the insurance money and retired. "And what would I do with it? Eat more? Buy another suit? Retire and die," asks Feuerstein. "No, that did not go into my mind."xxxi But he was determined to rebuild Malden Mills as a state-of-the-art facility.

Sadly, it was the high cost of rebuilding as a state-of-the-art facility, combined with changing market conditions, and not this generous act, that ended Mr. Feuerstein's tenure as chief of Malden Mills. David Gill observed:

> But the company carried substantial increased debt because of the high costs of re-building a state-of-the-art facility. The volatility of the textile industry hurt the company. Three warmer than usual winters in the late '90s depressed sales of cold weather fabric garments. The result was that Malden Mills declared bankruptcy in November 2001 and Feuerstein was replaced as CEO.[xxxii]

Sometimes even the best laid plans can go awry. And that was the case at Malden Mills. It was not Aaron Feuerstein's generosity that did him in. It was noted that, "In the immediate aftermath of the re-opening of Malden Mills product sales and employee productivity soared by some 40 percent."[xxxiii] It was debt and changing market conditions, a poor strategic foresight, which forced Mr. Feuerstein from his company. He could have just taken the insurance money and faded off into a retirement life of luxury and comfort for himself, but he didn't.

Contrast what Aaron Feuerstein did with what other CEOs are doing, as highlighted in a January 2012 MSNBC article:

> CEOs and other top executives of companies that go through Chapter 11 receive robust compensation in the form of salary, stock grants and other benefits. In some cases, they earn even more money than they did before the filing, even while other stakeholders suffer.[xxxiv]

Think about this: if you are in a position of leadership

simply to grab whatever rewards you can from your organization, no matter what the cost to anyone else, then you are not practicing true and effective leadership. And after you are gone from this earth, no one will care how about much money you made unless they are the heirs to your estate. The leadership of Aaron Feuerstein and Paul is celebrated years after their acts because they showed compassion for their fellow human beings regardless of the cost to themselves. That is what true and effective leadership is about.

Questions for Discussion or Contemplation

1. Which of Richard Daft's four leadership eras describes your style of leadership? Why do you practice your particular leadership style?

2. Do you agree or disagree with Aaron Feuerstein's decision to retain his employees while his factory was rebuilt? Why or why not?

3. Explain a time when you displayed compassion for one of your followers or employees. Was there a benefit to your organization as a result of your compassion?

4. How would Paul's mission have been impacted had he escaped from his prison cell that night and allowed his jailer to commit suicide?

CHAPTER IV: CONFLICT

Many people within organizations are understandably wary of engaging in any type of conflict. Conflict can lead to confrontation and confrontation can be stressful to the participants, ruin workplace relationships, and be considered time-consuming. Scholars Hocker and Wilmot said that conflict arises from "...the interaction of interdependent people who perceived incompatible goals and interference from each other in achieving those goals."[xxxv] Considering the potential for stress, hostility, and lost productivity, can conflict ever be considered as good for organizations? When handled appropriately, conflict can indeed be considered essential for organizations to grow, evolve, resolve, and innovate. What do I mean when I say "conflict handled appropriately"? That is what this chapter is about!

Paul was not a leader to shy away from conflict, even when he knew what he said would get him arrested and thrown in prison. He would even engage his fellow disciples if he felt that there was an issue with what they needed to do to advance their mission of spreading the Gospel. It was because of a conflict that Paul dissolved his partnership with Barnabas as the two of them were planning a mission trip together. The Book of Acts recorded, "Barnabas wanted to take along John, whose other name was Mark. But Paul did not want to, because Mark had left them in Pamphylia and had stopped working with them" (Acts 15:37-38). So Paul wanted to concentrate on the work at hand and not have to worry about whether Mark would desert them mid-mission again, whereas Barnabas was willing to forget Mark's transgression and press on with him.

Apparently both men stood their ground and ended up going their separate ways. "Barnabas took Mark and sailed to Cyprus, but Paul took Silas and left after the followers had placed them in God's care. They traveled through Syria and Cilicia, encouraging the churches" (Acts 15:39-41). One could say that the conflict was bad because it cost Paul and Barnabas their partnership. On the other hand, it was good for their organization because, instead of one mission trip going out, there were two. And thus, this was a situation where a conflict helped an organization to move forward.

Think for a moment how conflict works within *your*

organization. You may want to consider avoiding it whenever possible. As I stated earlier, conflict is stressful. Would it not just be nicer if everyone at work simply agreed with each other? There would be no arguments, no tension, with all employees doing what they do so that the organization can move along smoothly. Wouldn't that be great? Not so, in my opinion, and hopefully not in yours, either. There's a word for the kind of utopia I've just described. That word is *groupthink*, and it has the potential to bring your organization to a grinding halt, and possibly kill it.

The problem with having everyone in a leadership group constantly getting along is that everyone is so busy getting along that problems and opportunities pass them by. Nahavandi explained:

> This homogeneity in top management teams and board membership caught the blame recently for many of the problems in U.S. businesses. Industrial giants such as General Motors, AT&T, and IBM suffered from the lack of initiative and creativity of their top management teams. The members worked well together and disregarded input from outsiders. As a result, they failed to foresee the problems and full consequences of their decisions or inaction.[xxxvi]

This almost sounds like the organization is being run by a bunch of pre-teenagers with a tree fort who don't want to let the new kid in town in to join them, only to find out after they ticked the new kid off that his dad was planning to buy pizza for everyone. With that in mind, think about what kind of group is running the show at *your* organization!

Let us look at another possible scenario. According to

Eisenberg, Goodall, and Trethewey, whenever a group or a team comes together to make decisions regarding the organization, some members of the team may dominate the others in an attempt to get their ideas across and grab power. When the others in the team allow another member to dictate the group's decisions in order to keep the peace, it is referred to as "groupthink."[xxxvii] The problem with groupthink is that not every idea gets heard within the group, so if a proposed idea has a flaw, the person who spots that flaw keeps quiet about it so as not to cause conflict within the group. That can explain how bad ideas become policy.

When I was a boy, I had a fascination that continues to this day with the Universal Studios monster movies of the 1920s, -30s, and -40s. I particularly liked the Frankenstein and Wolfman films. But one thing nagged at my subconscious whenever I watched those movies: Was I supposed to be more afraid of the monster or the single-minded angry mob that was chasing after it with torches and pitchforks? It looked to me like the mobs caused more damage than the creature they were pursuing. Too often, I would hear a line like, "The monster is trapped. Let's burn down the castle!" With that in mind, what kind of damage could a single-minded group cause to your organization?

The term "groupthink" was devised by Irving Janis in 1972 and warned that organizational teams are, "...especially vulnerable to groupthink when its members are similar in background, when the group is insulated from outside opinions, and when there are no clear rules for decision making."[xxxviii] The implication of groupthink is that the "yes people" are running the institution.

The exact method used for dealing with internal organizational conflict depends upon the situation and the individuals involved. But under no circumstances should conflict be simply ignored. The point of conflict is to come to a resolution. In order to resolve a conflict, authors Arthur Bell and Dayle Smith recommend that leaders use disarming phrases, such as, "Tell me how you see the problem," "I want to know your feelings about the situation and how you think we can get back on track," and "In your view, what can I do to help resolve the problem? What can you do?"[xxxix] The most important thing you, as leader, can do when people have an issue in conflict is to listen to them. After you listen, then you can weigh the benefits of possible solutions.

One example of a modern-day leader who did not run away from conflict was Anne Mulcahy, CEO of Xerox Corporation. In fact, what she did was walk herself right into what could have been a virtual hornet's nest of conflict. Anne Mulcahy took over as CEO of the then-troubled Xerox Corporation in August 2001.[xl] Richard Daft recalled, "When she made the difficult decision to close the struggling personal computer division, Mulcahy personally walked the halls to tell people she was sorry and let them vent their anger."[xli] This was a situation in which the CEO of an organization, the person who made the decision to close a division and lay off the employees, walked right into the halls of that division and allowed those employees to get in her face! Suddenly the conflicts going on at your organization may not seem so bad anymore!

Richard Daft explained, "Face-to-face communication with followers during difficult times is crucial for good leadership. People want to know that their leaders care about them and what they're going through."[xlii] Unfortunately, this is an era where top leaders are difficult to find when their employees are being informed that they are being laid-off via an email.[xliii] Conflict can be a good thing for your organization due to "...its role in generating different ideas and perspectives...as well as in facilitating the sharing of information."[xliv] If a leader such as Anne Mulcahy can face conflict with the very people she had decided to lay off, do you not think that you can easily face any conflict that would occur in your organization?

Questions for Discussion or Contemplation

1. Describe how disagreements and conflict are commonly handled within your organization. Does your organization benefit or not from its handling of conflict?

2. Does excessive cooperation or "groupthink" exist within your organization? What is happening within your organization as a result?

3. Can you think of a movie that describes the conflict management style at your organization? Which movie is it and why did you choose it?

4. Put yourself in Anne Mulcahy's shoes. You have just issued the order to lay off a group of employees. How would you deliver the news to them?

CHAPTER V: CHARACTER

Magazine publisher Malcolm Forbes said, "You can easily judge the character of a man by how he treats those who can do nothing for him."[xlv] Another common paraphrase in American organizational culture is, "Character is about doing the right thing for the right reason even if there is no one else around to see you do it." How does that sentiment work for you within your organization? Are you always doing the right thing, not to show everyone that you did it, but because doing that right thing is essential to your core beliefs? And what if your doing that right thing is unpopular or got you into trouble?

Would you still do it? Character is who we are deep down inside, and it affects every single one of our actions.

Paul showed us his character by sticking to his ministry, his task at hand, regardless of the personal cost to himself, even when it meant he would be beaten and thrown in prison. In chapter three of this teaching, we discussed how Paul and his ministry partner Silas, while in prison, saved the life of their jailor. The reason they were in that prison in the first place was because Paul had helped a slave girl by driving out a demon that possessed her. The Book of Acts recorded:

> One day on our way to the place of prayer, we were met by a slave girl. She had a spirit in her that gave her the power to tell the future. By doing this she made a lot of money for her owners. The girl followed Paul and the rest of us and kept yelling, "These men are the servants of the Most High God! They are telling you how to be saved." This went on for several days. Finally, Paul got so upset that he turned and said to the spirit, "In the name of Jesus Christ, I order you to leave this girl alone!" At once the evil spirit left her. When the girl's owners realized that they had lost all chances for making more money, they grabbed Paul and Silas and dragged them into court (Acts 16:16-19).

Paul did the right thing by ordering the spirit out of the slave girl; however, we are left with the question as to why he waited several days before he did it. It is possible that the issue was timing and Paul and Silas needed to complete other tasks before they did something that would most likely get them arrested and thrown in prison.

By the time of this event, Paul had already been stoned to near death in Lystra (Acts 14:8-20), so the potential penalties for his ministering were well known to him. He kept to his mission even though he knew that at any time he could be arrested, whipped, stoned, imprisoned, or executed. Paul knew that what he was doing was right, although in some circles it was not popular. He showed his character as he carried on despite any harsh cruelties that awaited him.

There appears to be a serious crisis in leadership these days. In recent years, multiple leaders have fallen due to issues relating to their character. Leaders are expected to show people the way to a better tomorrow. Do any of us really want that tomorrow to include marital infidelity, lying, taking rewards that are not deserved, or wallowing in self-pity when trouble strikes? Theologian Howard Hendricks once said, "The greatest crisis in the world today is a crisis of leadership, and the greatest crisis in leadership is a crisis of character."[xlvi] Leaders who attempt to tell their followers to behave one particular way while they themselves behave in an opposite and inappropriate way will be seen by those followers as ineffective leaders or, worse, hypocrites. Put yourself in the position of your followers. Would you want to work for anyone who said to act with integrity, but lacked integrity themselves?

Author and scholar Dave Kraft published a list of 15 positive traits necessary for good leadership character. Take a look at them and see how many you can honestly claim as your own. They are: "Gentleness, transparency, forgiveness, tactfulness, patience, dependability, thankfulness, vulnerability, honesty, trust, compassion, encouragement, humility, affirmation, and self-control."[xlvii] For anyone who wants to be remembered as a great leader, these traits are essential. If any of these traits do not apply to you, well, now you know what you have to work on.

Kraft went on to ask two important questions: "Can we really accomplish anything of value without the trust-filled collaboration of others? And can there ever be trust without solid character?"[xlviii] Here is something for every leader to think about: you would never enter a business relationship with someone you did not trust. If you, as a leader, are without dependability, honesty, compassion, humility, and self-control, then how can you expect anyone to trust you? Always look to do the right thing and you, too, may be remembered as a great leader.

Unfortunately, doing the right thing, for leaders, means that you occasionally have to fire someone from your organization. What if the person that should be fired is you? How would you handle that type of situation? The modern-day leader being spotlighted in this chapter made an unfortunate mistake, he held himself accountable, and sent himself packing.

His name is Devon Edwards, and in January 2012 he was the 21-year-old managing editor of Onward State, the online blog site of Penn State.[xlix] On Saturday, January 21, Onward State erroneously reported on its Twitter account that the then-former Penn State football coach Joe Paterno had passed away.[l] Shortly after the post was made, CBS Sports ran with the story, which prompted a response from members of the Paterno family, stating that Coach Paterno was still alive and fighting to stay that way.[li] Onward State had jumped the gun and ran with a major news headline that had turned out to be false. To make the matter worse, a major news organization had also reported on the inaccurate story and cited Onward State as the source.[lii] Consider that the reputations of both news organizations could suffer serious harm as a result of spreading a story that was untrue. Additionally, Joe Paterno's family was most likely further upset during a difficult time that the media was already reporting a death that had not yet happened. Who will be held accountable?

Devon Edwards decided that he, as the managing editor of Onward State, would hold himself accountable for the error. Mr. Edwards also decided that his penalty would be his own termination from the staff of Onward State. In a letter he composed later that very evening of January 21, 2012, Mr. Edwards wrote:

> Earlier this evening, Onward State reported that Joe Paterno had passed away; however, the mountain of evidence stacked opposite that report became too much to ignore. At this time, I would like to issue an official retraction of our earlier tweets... To all those who read and passed along our reports, I sincerely apologize for having mislead you. To the Penn State community and to the Paterno family, most of all, I could not be more sorry for the emotional anguish I am sure we at Onward State caused... I will be stepping down from my post as Managing Editor, effective immediately. I take full responsibility for the events that transpired tonight, and for the black mark upon the organization that I have caused.[liii]

There it was, and there it ended. He did not stonewall. He did not take a few weeks off to get his thoughts together. He did not make excuses for what happened. He certainly did not say things like, "It depends on what the meaning of the word 'is' is."[liv] Mr. Edwards apologized for what was done, took personal responsibility, and then he resigned.

Maybe reporter Kim Bhasin observed correctly when she wrote, "Did he need to resign? Perhaps not. Either way, it's sincere, heartfelt and human. There are no conditions set, no distancing and no excuses. He screwed up, and he accepted full responsibility."[lv] Coach Paterno passed away the following morning, and by then Mr. Edwards's tenure at Onward State was history.

Devon Edwards was only 21 at the time. All over the world there are monarchs, presidents, prime ministers, and CEOs who could learn an important lesson from his example about taking responsibility for what happens on your watch. Paul demonstrated to us that good character involves doing what one considers the right thing. Devon Edwards has demonstrated to us that good character can still set an example for others, many centuries after Paul.

Questions for Discussion or Contemplation

1. Think back to a time you did something that was unpopular with others. What was it that you did and what was the overall result of your action?

2. Do you agree or disagree with Devon Edwards's decision to resign from his position as editor of Onward State? Why do you feel that way? What, if anything, would you have done differently in this circumstance?

3. What do you see as possible reasons for Paul waiting several days before driving the demon out of the slave girl?

4. Review the Kraft list of good leadership character traits. Which one do you consider to be your weakest of the traits? What will you do now to strengthen it?

5. If a situation warranted it, would you be able to fire yourself?

CHAPTER IV: SERVICE

Much is being written in the modern-day news media concerning the subject of freedom: the freedom to do what we want, whenever we want, with whomever we want, no matter what it is that we want. But is focusing on ourselves truly a desirable trait? Is it not true that we are happiest when we are serving others? Possibly some folks in the retail profession may argue against the latter question, but consider the big picture via this quote from Paul, found in Galatians:

> Don't use your freedom as an excuse to do anything you want. Use it as an opportunity to serve each

other with love. All that the Law says can be summed up in the command to love others as much as you love yourself. But if you keep attacking each other like wild animals, you had better watch out or you will destroy yourselves (Galatians 5:13-15).

Paul said quite a bit in just those few sentences. The command to "love others as much as you love yourself" (Galatians 5:14) has its origin in the Ten Commandments, and was confirmed by Jesus (Mark 12:31). And history shows that, when we attack others, the results can indeed be costly.

Paul goes on to roll out an inventory of decadent ways people serve themselves rather than others. He wrote:

They worship idols, practice witchcraft, hate others, and are hard to get along with. People become jealous, angry, and selfish. They not only argue and cause trouble, but they are envious. They get drunk, carry on at wild parties, and do other evil things as well (Gal. 5:20-21).

Have you, as a leader, ever done any of these things and had it backfire on you? Well, Paul is trying to offer a blueprint for your success. You cannot do any of the things on his list and expect to be seen as an example for others to emulate. Paul concluded, "I told you before, and I'm telling you again: No one who does these things shall share in the blessings of God's kingdom" (Gal. 5:21). As you reflect on this last statement from Paul, realize that, while this project is presented from a Christian perspective, it is not meant exclusively for Christians. The Bible can be seen as the greatest organizational how-to book ever written, regardless of your eternal worldview.

Let us examine Paul's earlier statements. "Don't use your freedom to as an excuse to do anything you want" (Gal. 5:13). In effect, he said: Can we all agree that not everything that we want to do is good for us? Being myself a chocoholic, I know that I have the freedom to eat an entire one-pound bar of Belgian dark chocolate in one sitting. I have that freedom to do what I want. Who is going to stop me? Oh, yes...my wife! However, I happen to be aware that eating all that chocolate in one sitting will make me feel sick. So why would I do it? Being self-serving is often not good for us.

On the other hand, if I serve another person, how would that make me feel? Again, Paul wrote, "All that the Law says can be summed up in the command to love others as much as you love yourself" (Gal. 5:14). Suppose I take the money I was going to use to buy that giant bar of chocolate and I give it to a food bank, so that someone who is hungry and does not have the means can have something to eat. Or I buy a toy and give it to a child whose parent is in prison or on deployment. How would that make me, or you, feel inside? It would feel pretty good, right?

Yes, we have the freedom to do what we want, whenever we want, with whomever we want, no matter what it is we want. But, as leaders, we are called upon to set the example for others to follow. Instead of always thinking of what we want, we have to consider being of service to others. That is not easy. Leadership frequently is not easy. If it was, everybody would be doing it!

Most everyone can recall working for a leader they did not care for. Many leaders fail because they do not reach out to connect with their followers. The opposite of service to others is service to self, also known as narcissism. To be self-serving is not a desirable trait in a leader. It is true, though, that some globally-known leaders were, or are, narcissists. Is that the type of leadership you want to be known for? Some traits of narcissism are: "self-importance, arrogance, inability to tolerate criticism, a sense of entitlement, exploiting others, and a lack of empathy for others."lvi Leaders who exhibit those characteristics, whether they operate on a localized or global scale, will be unlikely to inspire their employees to put forth their very best efforts for the organization. And if you lead a staff of volunteers that you do not have a paycheck with which to inspire them, do not expect them to stay with you for very long.

Are leaders themselves responsible for when they fail? They can be! In addition to narcissism, Nahavandi wrote that some common characteristics of leaders who failed include, "Coldness or arrogance; poor communication; untrustworthiness; an abrasive, intimidating style; poor communication, and an inability to delegate."lvii What do all of these characteristics have in common? They are all personality flaws that can be dealt with, if the leader chooses to. Leaders may worry that they will not be remembered if they are serving-others oriented. But they will most certainly be remembered, and most likely not in a good way, if they are self-serving.

Take a moment to consider the words of the greatest of leaders, Jesus of Nazareth. He said, "If you want to be great, you must be the servant of all the others. And if you want to be first, you must be the slave of the rest. The Son of Man did not come to be a slave master, but a slave who will give his life to rescue many people" (Matthew 20:26-28). During His time on earth, Jesus could have had the world at his feet. Instead, He washed the feet of others. He could have been born into the richest of families. Instead, He was born in an animal shelter. He could have enjoyed all the admiration and accolades that the first century had to offer. Instead, He chose to sacrifice Himself on the cross. I speak to leaders the world over when I say: if Jesus can do this for all the people of the world, what can you do for the people under your supervision?

Like Devon Edwards, who was profiled in chapter five, this modern-day leader also terminated her own position. But her reason for terminating herself was very different from that of Mr. Edwards. Lola Gonzalez owned her own company, Accurate Background Check, located in Ocala, Florida. As the owner, she was paying herself a six figure salary.lviii "The firm does background checks of job applicants and screens tenants, among other services."lix However, at the start of the economic downturn in 2008, her business began to decline. Ms. Gonzalez's husband looked over the company books in March of 2010 and told her that she would have to lay off one of her employees. She said her employees initially laughed when she told them she was laying herself off.lx Consider this situation: Lola Gonzalez is not a hired manager...she owns the organization...and she terminated herself! Who does that?

Who was left behind to run Ms. Gonzalez's business? She told her remaining employees, "You are. You are, and I trust you."lxi Paul said, "...love others as much as you love yourself" (Galatians 5:14). By giving up her own job and salary in order to save the job of one employee, Ms.

Gonzalez had truly displayed her love for others. Ms. Gonzalez explained, "We provide wise hiring decisions, I mean, information for employers to make the wise hiring decisions. As I hired them, I was confident I was doing the right thing."[lxii] Through her connections, Ms. Gonzalez was able to quickly secure another job for herself, though at a much lower rate of pay.[lxiii] She and her family had decided to forego some luxuries as a result of her new situation.

If you were an employee at Ms. Gonzalez's company at the time of this layoff, how would you feel about working for this leader? Bruce Winston wrote, "Loyalty and devotion to task and company grow out of trust and the knowledge of protection that comes from the employment relationship. Employees who know that the leader has their interests at heart are willing to commit themselves to corporate tasks."[lxiv] Lola Gonzalez focused on what was best for others, not for herself. She provided her employees with the ultimate service, the ultimate sacrifice. Using your freedom as "an opportunity to serve each other with love" (Galatians 5:13) was what Paul said. If he were standing among us here today, I think he would agree that Lola Gonzalez did just that...and that she is a great leader.

Questions for Discussion or Contemplation

1. Can you think of any leaders from history who used their positions to serve themselves rather than their followers? Who are they and what are they most remembered for?

2. Can a self-serving leader ever turn into a leader who serves others? What would they need to do?

3. Think of a time that you used your leadership position to help someone else. What did you do for that person? How can you use your position to help others in the near future?

4. Have you ever worked for a leader who served themselves? What did they do, or not do, that made their self-service evident? Is that leader still in a position of leadership?

5. What will you be doing differently within your position of leadership as a result of reading this book?

CONCLUSION

There are certainly many lessons within the life and writings of Paul the Apostle for people in positions of leadership to contemplate. With so many leaders coming under fire for committing acts of lust, greed, and cruelty, it would appear that these are dark times for the art of leadership. But the purpose of this endeavor is to inspire great leadership. Oscar Wilde once said, "Every saint has a past and every sinner has a future." Every leader has the potential for a great future, regardless of their past. Paul had blood on his hands, and look at all he managed to do after he answered his ultimate call into service. But you have to make a decision to lead as a great leader. Has Paul yet inspired you to become a great leader? Will you be doing anything differently as a result of Paul's example, or of the examples of the other leaders presented in these lessons?

The overall point of this series is for leaders to treat others the way they would expect to be treated themselves. Consider this other writing from Paul, where he wrote: "Slave owners, be fair and honest with your slaves. Don't forget that you have a Master in heaven" (Colossians 4:1). It is hopefully preferable to think that no one following these words in this modern day actually owns slaves. It is also possible that not everyone following these lessons is a believer in the Lord. So, by taking the liberty of changing a few words in Paul's statement, a lesson is created that is applicable to all modern-day leaders: leaders, be fair and honest with your followers. Don't forget that you also are accountable to someone.

Let us take a look at all that was covered in this teaching. In chapter one, humility was spotlighted as a valuable trait for leaders. Servant-leadership, where the leader moves their organization forward by helping the followers, allows leaders to make great impression that will be remembered. Next, contentment was considered as a means to organizational productivity. Leaders set the emotional tone in their place of work, and chaos is not conductive to proper employee motivation. Give your employees a sense of peace so that they can focus on their organizational tasks. Chapter three talked about the importance of compassion in a leader. Make sure that your followers know that you care about them, and they will have a good reason to care about you and the organization. How can your organization thrive amidst unresolved conflicts?

Chapter four encouraged leaders to tackle the challenge of conflict in order to bring about resolutions, and then move forward with the business of the organization. Beware of constant like-mindedness or groupthink, which can stagnate or kill an organization. Character, as discussed in chapter five, is who each of us really are deep, down inside. Do you find that your character has you looking out for the good of all those around you...or just you? Your followers are watching to see what your priorities are. Finally, chapter six valued the trait of service. Leaders are much more likely to be remembered as great leaders if they put their talents to use in serving others. Leaders who are self-serving will most likely be remembered as such.

Following in the footsteps of the first Christian martyr, Stephen, who decades earlier died with Paul's blessing, Paul himself paid the ultimate price for his way of life. The Book of Acts recorded that Paul's final arrest was the result of a mistaken belief by the Jews that Paul had brought a Gentile into the Temple (Acts 21:27-29). At the time, such an act was considered a violation of Jewish law. As the Roman citizen that he was, Paul requested to be tried by the Emperor of Rome, rather than be handed over to the Jews (Acts 25:10-12). After a long journey that included being shipwrecked on the island of Malta (Acts 27:39-44, 28:1), Paul was brought to Rome. Following a couple of years of house arrest (Acts 28:30), he was executed by the Romans via beheading. In 2009, carbon dating on bones found inside the Tomb of St. Paul was conducted, and Pope Benedict XVI announced that, "This seems to confirm the unanimous and uncontested tradition that they are the mortal remains of the Apostle Paul." Since we obviously have no DNA samples known to be from Paul, carbon dating is the closest we will ever come to identifying his remains. Paul is long gone from this world, but the records of what he did and said remain to hopefully influence leaders all over the earth and throughout history.

Leaders who struggle with issues of how to conduct themselves within their positions of authority cannot simply defend themselves with excuses that other leaders are self-serving. In addition to Paul, six other leaders have been presented who took a higher path and paved a road to greatness for others to follow. Referring to the example of Jesus recorded in John 13, Lorin Woolfe wrote, "There is no scarcity of feet to wash. The towels and water are available. The limitation, if there is one, is our ability to get on our hands and knees and be prepared to do what we ask others to do." Are you willing to be that type of leader?

It is true that leadership positions can bring great rewards to some people. But please bear in mind that everything physical we have in this world, we have only temporarily. In about a hundred years from now, all of us will be dead and gone, and everything that we own will either be disposed of or belong to someone else. The only thing that will remain of you as a leader after you are gone will be your reputation. So the question that will be put to you is: how do you want to be remembered?

EPILOGUE

Will you now be doing anything differently in your leadership career as a result of reading this text? Will the lessons from Paul and the modern-day leaders that were presented inspire you to serve others rather than serving yourself? Can you be content, no matter what your present circumstances are, and share that contentment with those around you? Can you, as a leader, allow your actions to speak for you and forego unceasing self-promotion? What kind of lasting legacy can you leave by following the lessons of Paul?

History is littered with leaders who were self-serving or

did horrible things to their followers. We need more good examples of caring leaders. In addition to Paul, six other examples of great leadership were presented. Please do not become obsessed with the material rewards of leadership. You will not be taking them with you. As I wrote in an earlier chapter, upon your demise your possessions will either be disposed of, or ownership of them will be transferred to someone else. The only thing you get to keep after you are gone is your reputation.

About two months after I completed writing this text, a news story underscored the main message of *Business Leadership Lessons from Paul the Apostle*. A 69-year-old Nevada man had suffered from heart problems at home and passed away. It was after about a month that neighbors alerted authorities to check on him and his body was discovered.[lxv] Imagine the surprise of those authorities when they discovered that the man had stashed "gold bars and coins valued at $7 million"[lxvi] throughout his home. Apparently, the man's only rightful heir is a first cousin living in another state.[lxvii] Although the man had lived in the house for decades, neighbors knew very little about him. All they could say was that "he was quiet and not a problem."[lxviii] The gold is to be sold off and, after a tax payment to the IRS, the remaining proceeds will be turned over to the man's cousin.[lxix]

I consider this to be a very sad story. This man may have retreated from society, definitely hoarded a treasure, and, from what was made known, did nothing with it (I hope I am wrong about this, but no mention is made that he helped anyone with his money). Did he have a mental disorder that was responsible for his lifestyle choices? Since

"He never went to a doctor,"[lxx] no one will ever know. What we do know is that he is gone and that his legacy will be the treasure that was found in his house. That treasure now belongs to another person. It did nothing for the man when his end came.

It is never too late, as long as you are still breathing, to make changes to your life and become a leader who serves others. You can still be the effective leader with a reputation for getting things done. In fact, you may be even more effective because your people will work harder and smarter for you if they know that you have their interests at heart. Rather than spending their time figuring how to work around the leader's unpredictable mood swings, your people can solve the problems that will help your organization rise above your competition.

And when your time is done, people will remember you. Possibly as the demanding leader who always wanted the best from their people because of the great faith they placed in them, or as the leader who got the best from their people because they created an atmosphere within their office that allowed their employees to thrive. Paul has left instructions on how to effectively lead others. Although they may not realize it, other leaders are following Paul's example, and they are getting noticed. If you decide to follow Paul's example yourself, do not do it in order to intentionally get noticed yourself—Do it because you feel it is the right thing to do—and let history take care of the rest!

May God bless your efforts to effectively lead others.

ABOUT THE AUTHOR

Leo Wiltshire spent over two decades in assorted management capacities with a regional movie theater chain and a national retailer. Returning to school in 2008, he completed a Certificate of Graduate Studies in Church Leadership in August 2009 and a Master of Arts in Organizational Leadership degree in August 2012. Both the certificate and the degree were earned at Regent University. He lives in Virginia Beach, VA, with his wife, Eileen, and two cats who beg for attention whenever he sits down to write.

FOOTNOTES

[i] Daft, R. (2008). *The leadership experience* (4th Ed.). Mason, OH: South-Western. p. 4.

[iiii] McIntosh, G., & Rima, G. (2007). *Overcoming the dark side of leadership: How to become an effective leader by confronting personal failures.* Grand Rapids, MI: Baker Books. p. 40.

[iii] Sanders, E. (2009). *Paul.* New York, NY: Sterling Publishing Co., Inc. p. 15.

[iv] Oxford. (1996). *The Oxford dictionary and thesaurus, American edition.* New York, NY: Oxford University Press, Inc. p. 715.

[v] Spears, L. (2003). In R. Greenleaf. *The servant leader within: A transformative path.* Mahwah, NJ: Paulist Press. pp. 14–15.

[vi] Winston, B. (2002). *Be a leader for God's sake.* Virginia Beach, VA: Regent University School of Leadership Studies. p. 5.

[vii] Helman, C. (2011). Pay for America's highest-paid CEOs tops 131 million. *Forbes.* Retrieved Oct. 14, 2011 from http://www.msnbc.msn.com/id/44893005/ns/business-forbes_com/. Para. 3

[viii] Spears, L. (2003). In R. Greenleaf. *The servant leader within: A transformative path.* Mahwah, NJ: Paulist Press. p. 20.

[ix] Tanabe, K. (2011). Jarrett's general embarrassment. *Politico.*

Retrieved June 8, 2012 from
http://www.politico.com/click/stories/1102/valerie_jarretts
_general_embarrassment.html. para. 2.

[x] Rogers, R. (2011). Army vice chief of staff visits Fort Bragg.
Army.mil. Retrieved June 8, 2012 from
http://www.army.mil/article/53166/army-vice-chief-of-staff-
visits-fort-bragg/. para. 1.

[xi] Patterson, K. (2003). *Servant leadership theory*. Unpublished
document. Virginia Beach, VA: Regent University School of
Leadership Studies. p. 7.

[xii] Tanabe, K. (2011). Jarrett's general embarrassment. *Politico*.
Retrieved June 8, 2012 from
http://www.politico.com/click/stories/1102/valerie_jarretts
_general_embarrassment.html. para. 4.

[xiii] Winston, B. (2002). *Be a leader for God's sake*. Virginia Beach,
VA: Regent University School of Leadership Studies. p. 82.

[xiv] Blanchard, K., & Hodges, P. (2005). *Lead like Jesus: Lessons for
everyone from the greatest leadership role model of all time*. New York,
NY: MJF Books. p. 108.

[xv] Ibid.

[xvi] Winston, B. (2002). *Be a leader for God's sake*. Virginia Beach,
VA: Regent University School of Leadership Studies. p. 83.

[xvii] David, E. (2006). From Ace to the Almighty. *Christianity Today*.
March 7, 2006. Retrieved from
http://www.christianitytoday.com/ct/2006/marchweb-
only/fofshadyac.html. para. 3.

[xviii] Leitch, W. (2010). "Liar Liar" "Nutty Professor" director's life
has taken quite the turn. *Yahoo Movies*. Retrieved 11/17/2010
from http://blog.movies.yahoo.com/blog/133-liar-liar-nutty-

professor-directors-life-has-taken-quite-the-turn. para. 2.

[xix] Ibid. para. 3.

[xx] Casati, C. (2011). Tom Shadyac "I Am" is a journey of the heart. *The Epoch Times*. March 14, 2011. Retrieved from http://www.theepochtimes.com/n2/arts-entertainment/tom-shadyac-i-am-is-a-journey-of-the-heart-52828.html. para. 3.

[xxi] Hassett, S. (2011). Tom Shadyac wants you to wake up. *Esquire*. January 28, 2011. Retrieved from http://www.esquire.com/the-side/qa/tom-shadyac-i-am-012811.

[xxii] Ebert, R. (2011) I Am. *Chicago Sun-Times*. April 11, 2011. Retrieved from http://rogerebert.suntimes.com/apps/pbcs.dll/article?AID= /20110421/REVIEWS/110429996. para. 11.

[xxiii] Marshall, I. H. (2000). *Tyndale New Testament commentaries: Acts*. Grand Rapids, MI: IVP Eerdmans. p. 272.

[xxiv] Daft, R. (2008). *The leadership experience* (4th ed.). Mason, OH: South-Western. p. 21.

[xxv] Ibid. p. 22.

[xxvi] Ibid. p. 23.

[xxvii] Ibid.

[xxviii] Blanchard, K., & Hodges, P. (2005). *Lead/Like Jesus: Lessons for everyone from the greatest leadership role model of all time*. New York, NY: MJF Books. p. 99.

[xxix] Massachusetts Foundation for the Humanities. (2012). Fire destroys Malden Mills. *Mass Moments*. Retrieved from http://massmoments.org/moment.cfm?mid=355. Para. 1.

[xxx] Leung, R. (2009). Aaron Feuerstein—"The Mensch of Malden

Mills." *60 Minutes*. February 11, 2009. Retrieved from
http://www.cbsnews.com/stories/2003/07/03/60minutes/
main561656.shtml. para. 9.

[xxxi] Ibid. para. 8

[xxxii] Gill, D. (2011). Was Aaron Feuerstein wrong? *Ethix*. June 25,
2011. Retrieved from http://ethix.org/2011/06/25/was-
aaron-feuerstein-wrong. para. 4.

[xxxiii] Ibid.

[xxxiv] White, M. (2012). CEOs rake in huge sums when their
companies go bankrupt. *MSNBC*. January 27, 2012. Retrieved
from
http://bottomline.msnbc.msn.com/_news/2012/01/27/102
52581-ceos-rake-in-huge-sums-when-their-companies-go-
bankrupt. para. 2-3.

[xxxv] Lewicki, R., Saunders, D., & Barry, B. (2011). *Essentials of
negotiation*, (5th ed.). New York, NY: McGraw -Hill. p. 18.

[xxxvi] Nahavandi, A. (2012). *The art and science of leadership*, (6th ed.).
Upper Saddle River, NJ: Prentice Hall. p. 84.

[xxxvii] Eisenberg, E., Goodall, H., & Trethewey, A. (2007).
Organizational communication: Balancing creativity and constraint.
Boston, MA: Bedford/St. Martin's. p. 245.

[xxxviii] Psysr.org. (n.d.). What is Groupthink? *Psysr*. Retrieved
6/1/12 from
http://www.psysr.org/about/pubs_resources/groupthink%2
0overview.htm

[xxxix] Bell, A., & Smith, D. (2010). *Developing leadership abilities*, (2nd
ed.). Upper Saddle River, NJ: Pearson. p. 103.

[xl] Forbes.com. (2012). Anne Mulcahy. *Forbes*. Retrieved from
http://people.forbes.com/profile/anne-m-mulcahy/19732

[xli] Daft, R. (2008). *The leadership experience*, (4th ed.). Mason, OH: South-Western. p. 283.

[xlii] Ibid. P. 282.

[xliii] Associated Press, The. (2006). Radioshack fires 400 by email. *Seattlepi.com*. Aug. 31, 2006. Retrieved from http://www.seattlepi.com/business/283213_emaillayoffs31.html. para. 5-6.

[xliv] Eisenberg, E., Goodall, H., & Trethewey, A. (2007). *Organizational communication: Balancing creativity and constraint.* Boston, MA: Bedford/St. Martin's. p.248.

[xlv] Quote Investigator. (2011). You can easily judge the character of a man by how he treats those who can do nothing for him. *Quote Investigator*. October 28, 2011. Retrieved from http://quoteinvestigator.com/2011/10/28/judge-character/.

[xlvi] Kraft, D. (2010). *Leaders who last.* Good News Publishers/Crossway Books. Kindle Edition. p. 94.

[xlvii] Ibid. p. 102.

[xlviii] Ibid. p. 98-99.

[xlix] Vaccaro, C. (2012). Ward Melville alum resigns after Paterno death story. *Three Village Patch*. Retrieved January 22, 2012 from http://threevillage.patch.com/articles/ward-melville-alum-resigns-after-paterno-death-story. Para. 1.

[l] Bhasin, K. (2012). In Paterno death apology, a lesson for CEOs. *Business Insider*. January 22, 2012. Retrieved from http://www.msnbc.msn.com/id/46091333/ns/business-us_business/. para. 3.

[li] CBS Sports. (2012). Report: Paterno family weighs stopping ventilator. *CBS Sports*. January 21-22, 2012. Retrieved from http://www.cbssports.com/mcc/blogs/entry/24156338/344

97800. para. 1,2.

[lii] Ibid.

[liii] Bhasin, K. (2012). In Paterno death apology, a lesson for CEOs. *Business Insider.* January 22, 2012. Retrieved from http://www.msnbc.msn.com/id/46091333/ns/business-us_business/. para. 8,9,12.

[liv] Noah, T. (1998). Bill Clinton and the meaning of "is." *Slate.* Sept. 13, 1998. Retrieved from http://www.slate.com/articles/news_and_politics/chatterbox/1998/09/bill_clinton_and_the_meaning_of_is.html. para. 2.

[lv] Bhasin, K. (2012). In Paterno death apology, a lesson for CEOs. *Business Insider.* January 22, 2012. Retrieved from http://www.msnbc.msn.com/id/46091333/ns/business-us_business/. para. 15.

[lvi] Nahavandi, A. (2012). *The art and science of leadership,* (6th ed.). Upper Saddle River, NJ: Prentice Hall. p. 126.

[lvii] Ibid. p. 128.

[lviii] Davidson, P. (2010). Lola Gonzalez laid herself off to save her employees' jobs. *USA Today News.* November 25, 2010. Retrieved from http://tucsoncitizen.com/usa-today-news/2010/11/25/lola-gonzalez-laid-herself-off-to-save-her-employees-jobs/. para. 3.

[lix] Ibid. para. 8.

[lx] Ibid. para. 8-9.

[lxi] AP/CBS. (2010). With company facing job cut, woman fires herself. *CBS News.* Retrieved Nov. 27, 2010 from http://www.cbsnews.com/stories/2010/11/27/earlyshow/saturday/main7094344.shtml. para. 12.

[lxii] Ibid. para. 9.

[lxiii] Ibid. para. 16.

[lxiv] Winston, B. (2002). *Be a leader for God's sake.* Virginia Beach, VA: Regent University School of Leadership Studies. p. 29.

[lxv] Associated Press. (2012). Nevada man dies with $200 in bank, $7M in gold hidden inside home. FoxNews. Sept. 17, 2012. Retrieved from http://www.foxnews.com/us/2012/09/17/nevada-man-dies-with-200-in-bank-7m-in-gold-hidden-inside-home/?intcmp=trending#ixzz26onuiK71. para. 4.

[lxvi] Ibid. para. 2.

[lxvii] Ibid. para. 6.

[lxviii] Ibid. para. 11.

[lxix] Ibid. para. 8, 15.

[lxx] Ibid. para. 13.